THE CHANGING FACE OF
JAPAN

LEWIS LANSFORD and CHRIS SCHWARZ

HODDER
Wayland

an imprint of Hodder Children's Books

© 2002 White-Thomson Publishing Ltd

Produced for Hodder Wayland by
White-Thomson Publishing Ltd
2/3 St Andrew's Place
Lewes
BN7 1UP

Editor: Anna Lee
Designer: Christopher Halls at Mind's Eye Design, Lewes
Proofreader: Sarah Doughty
Additional picture research: Shelley Noronha, Glass Onion Pictures

Published in Great Britain in 2002 by Hodder Wayland,
an imprint of Hodder Children's Books
Reprinted in 2002

British Library Cataloguing in Publication Data
Lansford, Lewis
    Changing Face of Japan
    1. Japan - Juvenile literature
    I. Title II. Lee, Anna III. Japan
    952
ISBN 0 7502 3497 0

Printed and bound in Italy by G. Canale & C.S.p.A. Turin

Hodder Children's Books
A division of Hodder Headline Limited
338 Euston Road, London NW1 3BH

The website addresses (URLs) included in this book were valid at the
time of going to press. However, because of the nature of the Internet,
it is possible that some addresses may have changed, or sites may have
changed or closed down since publication. While the author, packager
and Publisher regret any inconvenience this may cause readers, no
responsibility for any such changes can be accepted by either the
author, packager or the Publisher.

Special thanks to Shiho Harumatsu,
Naoko Ikeda, Honami Kimura,
Kasaburo Kimura, Gill Marsden,
Heather Marsden, Yoko Nishina,
Ayako Sakata, Kiyomi Suzuki and
Hiroko Yamagoshi.

Acknowledgements

Text by Lewis Lansford. All photographs
are copyright Chris Schwarz, with the
exception of: Hodder Wayland/Steve
Benbow 3, 9 (top), 31 (bottom);
Popperfoto 22 (bottom). Statistics panel
illustrations are by Nick Hawken.
The map (page 5) is by Peter Bull.

Contents

1 The Ancient Capital

To the Japanese, Kyoto is the heart and soul of Japan. Although it is no longer Japan's capital city, it was the country's capital for more than 1,000 years.

In the year CE 793, the Japanese emperor Kammu decided to build a new capital for Japan. He planned the city carefully. It was to be 4.5 km from east to west and 5.2 km from north to south. It was to have wide, straight roads laid out on a grid. The city was built, and in CE 794, Kammu officially made it the capital of Japan. He named the city Heiankyo, but today it is known as Kyoto. It was Japan's official capital from CE 794 until 1868.

Tokyo is now the capital, but Kyoto is still a very important city. Its silk, pottery and other arts and crafts are considered the best in Japan. The city also has industry: chemicals, aircraft parts and electrical equipment are some of the goods made there. There are more than 2,000 ancient buildings in Kyoto, nearly 40 universities and colleges and more than 20 museums.

In Kyoto, monks perform ancient religious ceremonies in antique temples, but they also drive brand-new motorscooters and use the latest mobile phones. Kyoto has more historic buildings than any other Japanese city but it also has an ultra-modern train station. Kyoto has museums, but it also has factories. In Kyoto, the best of old Japan and the best of new Japan live side-by-side.

▲ *This man is wearing a traditional Japanese jacket called a haori. His mobile phone is the latest model.*

▶ *This woman, wearing a traditional kimono, is riding on a train in Kyoto. Japan's railways are among the most modern and efficient in the world.*

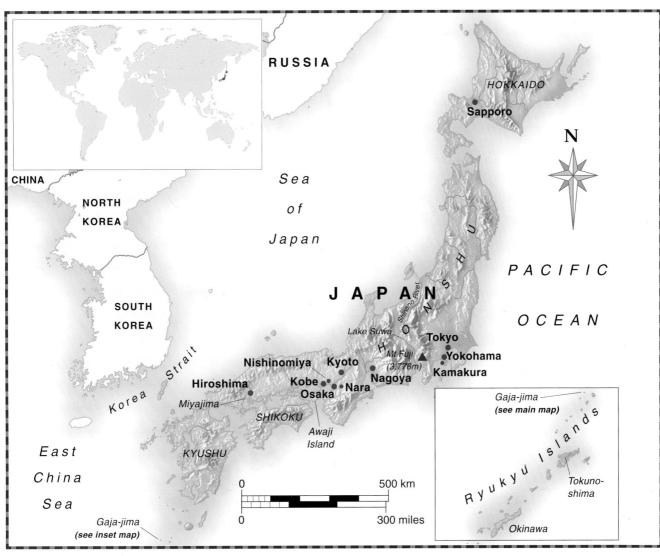

▲ This map shows the main features of Japan's landscape and the major cities.

Other places mentioned in this book are also shown.

JAPAN: KEY FACTS

Area: 377,708 sq km

Population: 125 million

Population density: 333 people per sq km

Capital city: Tokyo

Other main cities: Yokohama (3.2 million), Osaka (2.6 million), Sapporo (1.8 million), Nagoya (2.1 million), Kobe (1.5 million)

Highest mountain: Fuji (3,776 m)

Longest river: Shinano River

Main language: Japanese

Major religions: Buddhism, Shinto

Currency: Yen

In the early 1950s, about 40 per cent of the Japanese workforce was employed in agriculture, forestry or fishing. This began to change in the late 1950s. Japanese products such as cameras and motorcycles were becoming popular in other countries because of their reasonable price and high quality. Many people left other jobs to work in manufacturing.

As a result of this change, traditional agriculture, forestry and fishing became less productive. The government had to give rice farmers money just so they could afford to grow enough rice to feed the country.

By the 1970s, Japan's manufacturing economy was so strong, it was called an economic miracle. The Japanese became known for their hard work. In exchange for employees' dedication and loyalty, large companies were able to give full-time workers a job for life and to treat them fairly.

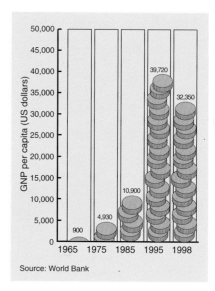

Source: World Bank

▲ *The amount of money Japan earns from the goods it produces increased rapidly between 1965 and 1995. In the late 1990s it began to decrease.*

▼ *Being a Buddhist monk requires hard work, dedication and study. Japanese people admire these qualities, and are very disciplined in their work. This has helped to make Japan's economy strong.*

IN THEIR OWN WORDS

'My name is Makoto Shibuya. I work for a manufacturing company in Itami, near Osaka. We make steel parts for cars. My job is to sell these parts to companies that manufacture cars. My average working week is about 70 hours. This doesn't leave much time for my hobbies. I like to practise karate and I also play the drums.

'Some of my friends don't have to work as hard as I do. Occasionally I think about finding a less demanding position so I could have more leisure time, but my company takes good care of me, and that's important, too. If I have kids, when they grow up, maybe they will come home from work earlier than I do!'

This has often not been the case in other countries, where many workers expect to change jobs frequently in life.

However, by the mid-1990s business had slowed. As a result a big change occurred: some Japanese companies occasionally had to make some of their employees redundant because there wasn't enough work. A job for life was no longer guaranteed. This trend has continued into the new millennium.

The end of guaranteed lifetime employment is having a deep effect on Japanese society. Young people who are starting work now are more interested in balancing work and relaxation than their parents were. Some people feel that if total devotion to work won't guarantee job security, they should enjoy more leisure time. Many Japanese are beginning to spend more time with their families and take longer holidays.

▶ *When these two students in Kyoto begin working, they probably won't work as hard as their parents did. For them, balancing work with fun is important.*

Landscape and Climate

Japan is made up of about 3,600 small islands clustered around the four larger islands of Honshu, Hokkaido, Kyushu and Shikoku. The islands have formed where two huge pieces of the earth's surface – called plates – are pushing against one another. Over time this led to pressure on the earth's surface and formed the steep mountains and deep valleys that make up 75 per cent of Japan's landscape.

Lakes and coasts

Japan's many islands have a total of 29,000 km of coastline. This is about three-quarters the length of the Equator! Steep mountains, volcanic activity and fast-flowing rivers have worked together to create many lakes, too. In prehistoric times, there was a huge lake at the foot of Mount Fuji, Japan's highest mountain, which is volcanic. Sometimes when the volcano erupted, lava flowed down the mountain and into the lake. Each time this happened, the lava cooled in the water, and created a dam that divided the big lake into smaller lakes. After this happened several times, the big lake had been turned into five smaller lakes. Now, as a group, they are called *Fuji Goko*, which means 'Fuji Five Lakes'.

▼ *Japan is surrounded by the sea, so the sea is an important part of all aspects of life in Japan. This gate at Miyajima, near Hiroshima, is called the Floating Torii. In the past it was used as an 'entrance' to a holy island off the shore of Honshu.*

Volcanoes

Japan has more than 200 volcanoes. The most famous is Mount Fuji, which stands at 3,776 m. On a clear day, Fuji can be seen from Tokyo, 100 km away. Fuji last erupted in 1707, covering the streets of Tokyo in a layer of ash.

Earthquakes

Japan has about 1,000 earthquakes every year. Most are too small to notice, but some are huge. One of Tokyo's biggest earthquakes ever was in 1923. It measured 8.2 on the Richter scale and killed 150,000 people. In 1995 an earthquake in Kobe measured 7.2 on the Richter scale and killed 6,300. Many died when their houses collapsed from the violent shaking of the earth. Houses built after the earthquake use the latest construction techniques to make them earthquake-resistant. For example, strong wooden frames are built into the walls in 'X' shapes that bend in an earthquake, but won't break.

▲ *Mount Fuji is sacred to many Japanese, a symbol of the nation and an inspiration to poets and artists for centuries.*

IN THEIR OWN WORDS

'I am Kasaburo Kimura. I live in Nishinomiya, near Kobe. This temple, near my house, was destroyed on 17 January 1995 in the Great Kobe Earthquake. The picture in the book I'm holding shows how it completely collapsed.

'Many houses in my neighbourhood were destroyed. When we re-built, the whole neighbourhood worked together. We made the roads wider – which is safer – and even built a park. Now the neighbourhood is modern. Before the earthquake, though, a lot of older people lived in the area. They didn't have enough money to rebuild, so now many of them live with their families in other places.'

Climate

From north to south, Japan covers nearly 25 degrees of latitude – about 3,300 km. Hokkaido, in the north, has short summers and long, snowy winters while the Ryukyu Islands in the south have long, subtropical summers and milder winters.

The four seasons

Japan has four clearly-defined seasons. In winter, icy winds blow off the Asian continent. The weather is cold, especially on the northwest side of Japan, which faces the Sea of Japan.

Spring usually begins when warm winds called monsoons begin to blow up from the South Pacific. The weather becomes milder. At the end of spring, a month of very rainy weather begins, usually in mid-June.

▼ *These primary-school children in Kamakura are on a school trip to see the cherry blossoms. The cherry blossom is an important sign of spring in Japan, and the entire nation celebrates its arrival.*

Summers are hot and humid in most of Japan, with temperatures in the mid-30s °C. In the northern island of Hokkaido, however, the weather remains cooler. This is a time when people like to travel to Hokkaido to escape the heat and humidity elsewhere.

Autumn begins with the arrival of big tropical storms called typhoons. Typhoons bring strong winds and heavy rains. As autumn draws to an end, the weather becomes cool, clear and dry – perfect for enjoying the dramatic colours of changing autumn leaves.

Climate change

Japan's climate is becoming warmer. Records dating back to 1443 show that in the old days, Lake Suwa, in central Honshu, was frozen for many months through each winter. Nowadays, the lake only freezes for short periods of time. Scientists believe that this is a clear sign of global warming.

▲ *It often rains in Japan, so no one leaves home without an umbrella during the rainy season.*

IN THEIR OWN WORDS

'My name's Erika Sawai. I go to school in Osaka. I'm 16 years old. My favourite season is winter. I think Japan's mountains are beautiful in winter. One of the best things about winter is skiing. I love going to the mountains to ski. I wonder if global warming is going to cause problems for Japan. We already know that the polar ice-caps are melting. All that water has to go somewhere. If the sea level rises, Japan may have some problems. We're surrounded by the sea! I think the weather in Japan is already becoming strange. The seasons seem all mixed up, with warm winters and cold springs.'

Natural Resources

Agriculture

More than 70 per cent of the food eaten in Japan is produced there. This is an amazing fact when you consider that the landscape is mostly steep hills and deep valleys. Only 13 per cent of the land can be farmed. Farms are small, less than 1.5 hectares on average. Because of this, Japanese farmers must make the most of the land they use. Japanese farming is becoming more efficient: the number of farmers is decreasing year by year, but the amount of food produced is remaining the same.

Rice is Japan's main staple food. No traditional meal is considered complete without it, so rice is the main crop. More than 40 per cent of the farmland is used to grow rice and rice from other countries rarely needs to be imported. Japan's other important crops are sugar beets, potatoes, cabbages, citrus fruits, sugar cane, sweet potatoes and onions. Apples, melons, soybeans, tea and tobacco are also grown.

Source: Geographical Digest

▲ The number of people working in agriculture in Japan has fallen dramatically since 1960.

Livestock

Pigs, cattle and poultry are raised on a small scale, but farm animals are not an important part of Japanese agriculture, because livestock takes up a lot of space. Near Kobe, a special kind of beef, called Kobe beef, is raised. It is considered some of the tastiest beef in the world. The cattle are given special treatment to make their meat tender, including regular massages and an unusual diet that includes beer.

◄ To grow rice, flat areas called terraces are cut into hillsides. These terraces are on Awaji Island.

IN THEIR OWN WORDS

'My name is Toru Tanaka. I live on a farm on Awaji Island. When I was a boy, 40 years ago, all of the work on my family's rice farm was done by hand or with simple tools. Now, I use a tractor, which means the work isn't as hard as it used to be. People are eating more and more bread in Japan now, which means that they're eating less rice. Still, rice is Japan's most important crop, and I feel proud to grow it.

'In the last few years, we've had some bad seasons. The weather has been too dry, so we weren't able to grow enough rice. We had to import rice from other countries. A lot of people said that the imported rice didn't taste as good as Japanese rice!'

Seaweed

Seaweed is a traditional part of the Japanese diet. It is grown in shallow water on undersea farms in the Sea of Japan in south-eastern Japan, along the north-eastern coast of Honshu and around Hokkaido. About 350,000 tonnes of one popular type of seaweed, called *nori*, are produced each year. The seaweed is planted in nets that are lowered from boats onto the bottom of the sea.

In the old days, the seaweed had to be harvested by hand as the nets were pulled up from the bottom of the sea. This was hard work, especially because the harvest takes place in winter. Nowadays, a petrol-powered cutter is used for harvesting, which makes the job much easier.

▲ *This woman is harvesting spinach on her farm near Kobe. As in much of Japan, the field is very small and close to tightly-packed houses.*

Minerals

Japan has a variety of mineral resources, including limestone, coal, copper, lead, zinc, natural gas and quartzite. There is not enough of any of these for the country's needs, so most of the minerals used in Japan need to be imported. Japan is the world's largest importer of oil.

Energy sources

Japan is one of the world's major electricity producers – and also a great consumer of electricity. About 65 per cent of Japanese electricity comes from coal- or petroleum-fed thermal plants, 23 per cent is nuclear and 12 per cent is hydroelectric. A tiny percentage of electricity is also produced by experimental wind farms. Use of nuclear power is increasing, to reduce the need for imported petroleum. In 1973, about 75 per cent of Japan's energy was generated by imported petroleum. This has been cut to about 55 per cent today.

▼ *It takes a lot of power to light all of these signs in Tokyo. Japan has recently considered turning them all off at midnight, to save electricity.*

IN THEIR OWN WORDS

'My name is Youhei Tanaka. I'm 13 years old. I live in Osaka. I know about the problem of global warming from television. Pollution from power plants may be part of the problem. Nuclear power doesn't pollute the air, so it might be a good source of energy in the future. The trouble with nuclear energy is that it can be dangerous in other ways. Radiation from nuclear waste can be a real problem. Maybe someone in Japan will invent an ecological way to produce energy.'

Fishing

Fish is the second most important part of the Japanese diet, after rice. The Japanese fishing fleet sails all around the world, using huge 'factory ships' to process and package the fish as soon as they are caught. The fish is sold in Japan and in many other countries. Fish that is caught closer to home is eaten fresh, often without being cooked.

Other ocean resources

Pearls are highly-prized gems and have been harvested from oysters living in the waters around Japan for centuries. Even today, many pearls are taken from oysters by divers who dive to the bottom of the sea holding their breath. Pearls are not the only reason for diving, though. Many people travel to Okinawa and its surrounding islands, in the far south-west of Japan, for recreational scuba-diving. The subtropical waters are warm and clear and teeming with fish, coral and even sunken ships.

▼ *This market stall in Osaka is selling both fresh and dried fish. The freshest fish have been caught only hours before being sold.*

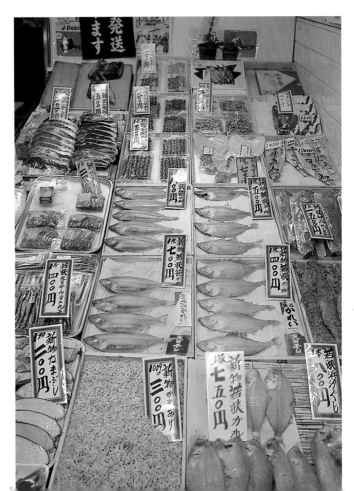

Forestry

Japan has many trees and produces a lot of wood. Wood is important for building, furniture-making and paper production. In recent years, the demand for wood in Japan has begun to decrease. There is more use of recycled paper products. For construction, building materials such as brick and concrete are being used instead of wood, or in addition to wood, to make buildings more earthquake-proof.

▶ *Bamboo has been used as a building material throughout Asia for centuries. It is still used today in some types of construction, but in Japan, it has been almost entirely replaced by manufactured materials.*

IN THEIR OWN WORDS

'My name is Norihiko Ikeda. I teach world history and Japanese history in a high school near the city of Nara. In this photograph I'm in my local hiking store. Japan is a small country, but more than half of it is mountainous. Because of this, we Japanese have a strong sense of connection to nature. Seeing the countryside makes us feel good. Going out and doing something in the countryside is even better! Skiing is one of my favourite sports. I love being surrounded by nature, by the mountains. In the old days, the Japanese people believed that God lived in the mountains. For the Japanese, it is very important for people and nature to co-exist – to live together. Even little parks, like we find in the city, can be seen as being part of nature.'

Other uses of the land

The central mountain range of Japan – the Japan Alps – has ten peaks that are over 2,000 m. In winter, the mountains are covered with snow and are perfect for skiing. Japan has more than 300 ski resorts. Most of them are on the island of Honshu, but the best skiing is in the north, on the island of Hokkaido. The ski season is usually from December to April. The 1998 Winter Olympics were held in Nagano, high in the Japan Alps.

Hot springs

Japan's constant volcanic activity heats underground water and creates another natural resource: hot springs. Japan has more than 2,000 hot springs, some of which come out of the ground at close to boiling temperature. Usually the water goes through extensive cooling to be the right temperature for bathing. Many people believe that hot springs can cure or prevent a variety of health problems, and everyone agrees that soaking in them is a great way to relax.

▲ *This park in the city of Kamakura makes it easy for city people to enjoy the feeling of the countryside.*

5 The Changing Environment

Japan's dramatic landscape is mostly steep mountains and deep valleys. As a result, cities have been built on the few available flat areas. As an increasing number of people have moved from the countryside to the cities, dealing with pollution has become a real challenge.

Air pollution

Cars, buses, lorries and factory chimneys pump poisonous gases into the air. The gases form brown clouds – called smog – that can damage your lungs and make your eyes sting. Air pollution may also be causing the Earth's temperature to increase.

Japan was one of the first countries in the world to introduce anti-pollution laws, and as a result air quality is better than it was twenty years ago. Cars and factories must be made to produce less pollution, and some factories recycle everything they use in manufacturing. Bathtub bases are made out of recycled plastic bags, bottle tops are used as construction material and cardboard boxes are turned into recycled paper. This means that fewer waste products are burned, and pollution is reduced. At the Kyoto World Climate Summit in 1997, more than 50 nations agreed that Japan and many other countries would try to reduce air pollution that may lead to global warming.

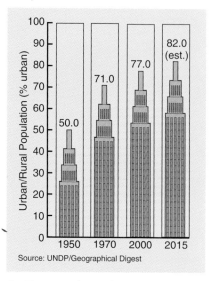

Source: UNDP/Geographical Digest

▲ The number of Japanese living in cities is still increasing.

◄ The city of Kobe is built on a narrow strip of land between the steep mountains and the sea. Like many cities in Japan, the large number of people living in a small area means that dealing with pollution can be difficult.

IN THEIR OWN WORDS

'My name is Ayako Sakata. I'm a high school teacher in Osaka. In geography, social studies and even English class, students learn about ecological problems – different kinds of pollution and the like. The students don't seem too concerned about these problems, but I suppose they are more interested than many adults are. I live in a suburb of Osaka. Noise pollution is really bad there, especially late at night. Young people on motorcycles make a real racket. The air in Osaka isn't very good, either. There is a lot of pollution from cars. We have solved one pollution problem. At the school where I work, some teachers used to smoke in the staff room. It smelt terrible. Now smoking is banned in the staff room.'

Water pollution

Factories and sewage plants sometimes put poisonous chemicals into rivers and the sea. This can cause people who use the water to become ill. After some bad cases of poisoned water causing serious diseases, Japan has worked hard to clean up rivers and the surrounding sea. River pollution has been steadily decreasing since the early 1980s. Pollution in lakes, marshes and bays, however, is still a problem. Some areas, including Tokyo Bay, have been set aside as special areas to be improved.

▶ *Japan's waterways and coasts have become badly polluted in the past. This sometimes meant that it wasn't safe to swim in the sea. These windsurfers are enjoying the clean waters in Kamakura.*

Light and noise pollution

Bright city lights make it impossible to enjoy looking at the stars at night and can make it difficult for drivers to see clearly. This is a type of pollution. Loud city noises can make it difficult for people to rest and relax, or to concentrate on work. This, too, is a kind of pollution. Complaints about noise and light pollution are increasing and it is likely that new laws will be introduced to control noise levels.

Recycling

Millions of tonnes of rubbish are created in Japan each day. With the limited land available, disposing of it all is a big problem. Burning it can cause air pollution, and dumping it into the sea can pollute the water. One way to help solve this problem is to recycle disposable household items such as glass and plastic containers and unwanted paper.

▲ *This is a busy street in Tokyo. Light and noise pollution are a big problem in Japan's cities.*

Throughout the country, household waste is separated by type and collected for disposal or recycling. Japan has one of the most efficient recycling programmes in the world.

There are other environmental problems that still need to be solved. People all over the world have protested because some Japanese fishing boats still use drift-nets. A drift-net is a fine net that is dragged between two boats. Sometimes, the drift-nets are as long as 50 km. They catch a lot of fish, but unfortunately, they also catch – and kill – many endangered species of turtles, dolphins, seabirds and sharks.

▲ *These bins for recycling materials are in the basement of a block of flats in Yokohama. People sort their rubbish by its material. Here metal is sorted into steel or aluminium.*

IN THEIR OWN WORDS

'My name is Honami Kimura. At my house in the city of Nishinomiya, we sort our rubbish very carefully. It's a big job, but I know it's good for the environment. We put different rubbish out on different days. Twice a week, we put out food waste and paper trash that can be burned. Once a week, we put out bottles and cans, in separate containers. Another day, it's plastic bottles. Twice a month, we put out newspapers and used boxes, and we also put out used clothes on this day. Oh, and I put our used tea leaves on my garden. It's a bit complicated!'

Land reclamation

One way to solve the problem of not having enough land is to make more land. This is a big job, but it can be done. Soil is taken from the mountain and placed in the sea. This creates a useful flat area on the mountain, and new, flat land in the sea. The new area might be an extension of the coastline, or it might be an island. This process is called land reclamation. Kansai International Airport, near Osaka, is built on an artificial island that is the size of 500 football pitches.

There are problems with land reclamation, however. When a mountain is removed, it destroys the plants that were living there and takes away animals' homes. The beauty of the mountain itself as part of the landscape is also lost. When an artificial island is built in the sea, it can stir up sand and soil in the water. When the soil settles again, it can smother living things such as coral. It may also cut down on the amount of sunlight that passes into the water and can reduce the number of fish in the area.

▲ *The city of Kobe has grown into the sea by moving earth from the mountains to extend the coastline.*

IN THEIR OWN WORDS

'My name is Shiho Harumatsu. I live with my husband and my daughter in a new apartment building in Yokohama. Compared to apartments in other countries, ours isn't very large. We don't have a garden, either. Even so, our small place is enough for us, and we are happy. Japan's cities are very crowded, so we have to make the most of the space we have. We are on the edge of a city, so it isn't so bad here. Our neighbourhood is clean and peaceful. We have a car, but parking it is a real problem. It's expensive to park it near the apartment. We use a special electric ramp that holds three cars – two of them underground – to save space!'

Whaling

In the middle of the twentieth century, whale meat was commonly eaten in Japan. Now, most countries in the world have agreed not to kill whales for food, because many types of whale are in danger of extinction. Japanese whale fishermen kill about 300 whales each year. The whalers say that it is for scientific research, to understand more about how whales' bodies work and how they live. However, almost all of the whales that are caught for research are then sold to be eaten. Many people think that the research is an excuse to kill whales for food. Also, the methods used to kill them are very cruel and painful for the animals.

Deforestation

Japan is heavily forested and does not have problems with deforestation. However, Japanese companies have cut down a lot of trees in other countries, such as Indonesia, for importing to Japan. In some cases, this has caused a lot of environmental damage.

▼ *These whalers are pulling their latest catch onto their ship.*

6 The Changing Population

There are about 125 million people living in Japan. 99 per cent are Japanese. The other 1 per cent are Korean, Chinese, Taiwanese and other nationalities. Compared with other countries, this is a small number of foreign residents. From about 1600 until the 1850s, Japan allowed almost no visitors from abroad, and most Japanese people were forbidden to travel to other countries. Almost no one outside of Japan could speak Japanese, and most Japanese people could speak only their own language.

In the twentieth century, communication with other nations increased. Now the number of foreigners in Japan is increasing. People come to Japan for a variety of reasons. Workers from Asia often come to work on building construction sites. Highly-skilled Indians are being encouraged to work in computer-related businesses in Japan.

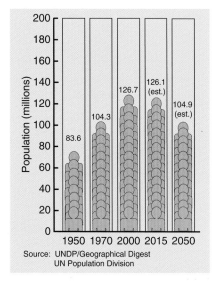

Source: UNDP/Geographical Digest UN Population Division

▲ *The population of Japan has been increasing for decades, but will soon start to fall.*

IN THEIR OWN WORDS

'My name's Karen. I'm from New Zealand. I first came to Japan when I was 19 years old, as a student. I've lived here for 8 years. My husband is Japanese. We have a business designing websites. I like living in Japan, because I can meet people from all over the world here. And the food! Not just Japanese food, but all kinds of food from all over the world is available here. I always wanted to learn Japanese pottery, so I started taking lessons. This photograph was taken during one of my classes. Japanese pottery is famous all over the world, and it has a very long history. It sometimes bothers me that it's so crowded here. Also, I'll always be seen as a foreigner. I can never become Japanese.'

People from all over the world come to study the Japanese language, martial arts, religion and traditional arts. Still others come to teach their own language – French, German, English, and so on – to Japanese students. Many foreigners work for Japanese companies that export products to other countries.

Japan's population is increasing very slowly. Experts predict that it will reach 127 million in the year 2007, and then begin to decrease. This is because fewer and fewer Japanese people are choosing to have children. By 2100, the population of Japan may be as low as 65 million. With 50 million fewer Japanese, Japan will almost certainly need more foreign workers in the future.

▼ This man from Israel is selling jewellery on a Tokyo street.

▼ Only 1 per cent of Japan's population is non-Japanese, so Westerners stand out in a crowd, even in Tokyo.

7 Changes at Home

Changes in marriage

As in most cultures, marriage and family have always been very important in Japan. For most of the twentieth century, more than 90 per cent of Japanese people married. Recently, however, that number has decreased as people choose to marry later in life. In 1970, fewer than 10 per cent of men in their 30s were still single, but now, more than 25 per cent remain unmarried.

In recent years, it has become more and more common for people in their 20s and 30s to continue living with their parents. Such people now make up 10 per cent of the Japanese population. In the past, they would have set up home with their husband or wife after marrying. Most of them have jobs, but many don't pay rent, do housework or cook for themselves – their parents do all of this for them. As a result, they have plenty of money to spend on luxury items such as personal computers, mobile phones and the latest hi-fi equipment. If these single people do marry and move away from home, they will have less money to spend on luxury items and having fun.

▲ *These young people in Tokyo would rather relax and enjoy life than take on the responsibilities of marriage.*

◄ *Some of the members of this wedding party in Kobe are wearing traditional Japanese clothes, while others wear modern clothes.*

IN THEIR OWN WORDS

'My name's Yoshihiro Kimura. I'm 17 years old. Of course I still live at home with my parents in Nishinomiya. They aren't too strict, so it's OK. I don't really have any plan to leave. Now, I'm doing a casual job for a removal company. It's not bad, but I'd like to earn more money. Big money. I have no idea how, though. Maybe I could start some kind of business. If I did earn a lot of money, I'd probably move out of my parents' house. I'm definitely not in a hurry to marry. Now is the time to play. When I'm 25, I might start thinking about marriage.'

Changes in birth rate

Because fewer people are marrying, the number of babies being born is decreasing. The average of two children per married couple is remaining stable.

Changes in religion

Almost everyone in Japan practises Shinto, Japan's ancient, native religion. It is based on the worship of nature and of ancestors. Most families take new-born babies to a Shinto shrine to be blessed by the priest. Japanese of all ages visit Shinto shrines to pray for things they want. University graduates pray for good jobs. Business people wish for the safety of their workers and for success in business.

Most Japanese are also Buddhists. Buddhism was brought to Japan from China in the sixth century CE. Many Japanese houses have Buddhist shrines where they keep photographs of loved ones who have passed away.

Christian missionaries brought their religion to Japan in the sixteenth century. Although only about 1 per cent of the Japanese are active Christians, many people choose to have a Christian-style wedding with a Christian priest or minister.

▼ *These new cans of soft drink have been left as an offering on this Buddhist statue. The tradition of leaving an offering of food or drink is a very old one.*

Changes in education

At the beginning of the 1990s, most Japanese schoolchildren had a six-day school week that included one half day of lessons on Saturdays. Now, due to changes introduced by the government, school on Saturday is becoming a thing of the past.

Nevertheless, Japanese students still have a reputation for working very hard at school. For students who hope to go to university, their junior high and high school years are full of long hours of study. Many students even attend classes at 'cram schools' in the evening, to cram in even more study. The university entrance exams are difficult and entrance into the best universities is very competitive. University life is said to be much easier than the tough years of exam preparation.

▼ *These students in Osaka stand up and bow when their teacher enters the room. It is both a greeting and a show of respect.*

IN THEIR OWN WORDS

'My name is Kumiko Matsui. I'm 17 years old. I'm in my last year of high school in Tokyo. I'm really busy! I go to school all day long, Monday to Friday, and my school still has classes two Saturdays per month. But that will end soon, and school will only be five days a week. I also go to a cram school at night. I want to pass my university entrance exams and go to a good university. I want to study English. I want to travel to other countries – you know, see the world. I guess more people speak English than Japanese, so I need to study English if I want to communicate. That shouldn't be hard, though. English is my favourite subject.'

In addition to the usual studies of maths, history, the sciences and of course Japanese language and literature, several years of English study is required by most schools. It is very common for students at college or university to further improve their English by taking courses in the United States or Britain as part of their studies. English has become the most common language of international business around the world, so it's important for people to be able to speak and understand it well.

▶ *These children are enjoying a religious festival at their local temple in Kyoto. Children often visit temples and shrines to pray for good luck with their studies.*

Changes in leisure

The changing expectations of workers and employers mean that the Japanese now have more leisure time than ever before. Every year, more and more Japanese people take holidays abroad. When they're relaxing at home, the Japanese use the latest televisions, stereos, video players and video game consoles, which are found in almost every Japanese home nowadays. The Japanese lead the world in the use of these sorts of electronic devices.

▼ *These surfers in Kamakura show that today's young Japanese know how to relax.*

Sports

Sports are very popular in Japan. Sumo wrestling is one of Japan's most popular traditional sports. The rules are simple: wrestlers try to push each other out of a 4.55 m diameter ring. Sumo wrestlers can be huge, and eat a special diet to gain weight and to maintain their big figure.

IN THEIR OWN WORDS

'My name's Tokowa Ogawa. I'm 17 years old. I go to school in Osaka. You won't believe this, but we don't have a TV at home. My father thinks talking with the family is more important. I guess we're the only people in Osaka without a television! I don't mind. Once in a while, I'll watch it at my grandmother's house. She lives close by. Anyway, I'd rather spend time with my friends than watch TV. They come over, and we talk and study in my room for hours. I like shopping a lot, too – for casual clothes, mostly. And I like going out to the cinema. I'll probably never buy a TV, even when I leave home. I like two-way communication. My latest hobby is sending e-mail!'

Judo, karate, and kendo are popular traditional martial arts that are often practised in school clubs.

Most people think of baseball as an American pastime, but it's also one of Japan's most popular sports. The Japanese started playing it at almost exactly the same time as the Americans, more than 120 years ago.

Soccer has become very popular since 1993, when Japan's soccer J-League was started. In 2000, the Japanese sent a team to the World Cup for the first time and Japan and South Korea hosted the 2002 World Cup. Golf is also very popular with business people.

Karaoke

Karaoke means 'empty orchestra'. It's popular all over the world, and was invented in Kobe in the 1970s. Karaoke singing is still more popular in Japan than anywhere else in the world; everyone seems to do it – business people, mothers, college students and primary school students.

▲ *Baseball is particularly popular with young people in Japan.*

Changes in health and medicine

Fast food is one type of foreign food that is becoming increasingly popular in Japan. With its fat and grease, fast food is beginning to cause the same health problems in Japan that it causes in other parts of the world: obesity and heart disease.

The traditional Japanese diet is very low in fat. This may be one reason why the Japanese, as a nation, live longer than almost anyone else in the world. Men live an average of 76 years, while women live an average of 82 years.

The traditional Japanese diet is not perfect, though. It contains a lot of salt, in the form of soy sauce and pickled foods. Eating too much salt can cause cancer, especially in the stomach. Smoking, which is very common in Japan, can also cause cancer and other health problems. Cancer is the main cause of death in Japan.

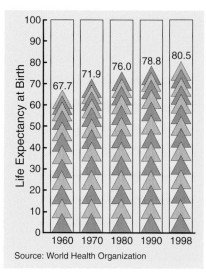

Source: World Health Organization

▲ Although changes in lifestyle mean that some new health problems are developing in Japan, the life expectancy of the Japanese is still increasing.

◄ Traditional pickled foods like these are very popular, but can cause some health problems.

Some health problems, such as stomach ulcers and heart disease, are caused in part by worrying too much and working too hard. An increase in leisure activity may help reduce some of these stress-related health problems in the future.

Medical care in Japan is of a high standard and it is available to everyone. Traditional Chinese medicine has been practised in Japan for thousands of years, and is still very popular. A modern doctor usually gives the same cough medicine to everyone who has a cough. A doctor of traditional Chinese medicine, however, gives different, special mixtures of herbs and other natural ingredients to each patient. Rather than try to stop the cough, a traditional Chinese doctor tries to restore the body to balance and health.

▶ *The proportion of old people in Japanese society is increasing as the birth rate decreases.*

IN THEIR OWN WORDS

'I'm Yasumasa Kikuoka. I'm a specialist in traditional medicine in the city of Nara. Traditional medicine uses ways of healing people that were developed thousands of years ago. I work in a shop that sells traditional herbal medicines – medicines made from plants. The shop is very old. It's been in the same location for more than 800 years! Of course Japan has some of the most modern hospitals in the world and all of the latest medicines, but many people think herbal medicine is more natural. In Japan, people are used to seeing a lot of very new things and very old things close together. This means that people sometimes use traditional herbal medicines, which are very effective for some medical problems, and sometimes use modern medicines, which are more effective for other problems.'

Changes in diet

Perhaps the most famous Japanese food is *sushi*, raw fish served together with rice. Fish has long been an important part of the diet, as the country is surrounded by ocean. The traditional Japanese diet does not include many dairy products such as milk, cheese and butter. The soy bean is often used in place of dairy products. *Tofu*, which is something like set yogurt, is made from soy beans, and so is soy milk.

A traditional home-made breakfast will usually include rice, a raw egg, fish and a bowl of clear soup called *miso*. For lunch, a businessman will traditionally have a box lunch, or *o-bento*, made especially by his wife. It will probably include rice, fish, and pickled fruit or vegetables. For dinner, rice, fish, noodles, beef, pork or chicken are common.

Food from other countries is becoming more popular in Japan. In Japan's main cities, it is possible to find a restaurant serving almost any kind of food you can imagine.

▼ *These girls in Kamakura are enjoying a traditional meal at a low table. Many Japanese families sit on the floor, at this type of table, to eat meals at home.*

◀ *This meal looks delicious, but you wouldn't want to eat it. It's a plastic imitation used to show people what's being served inside the restaurant.*

IN THEIR OWN WORDS

'My name's Seiya Moritani. I'm 9 years old. I live in Yokohama. For breakfast this morning, I had rice, *natto* – that's fermented soy beans – a fried egg and Japanese tea. Delicious. School lunch was good, too. I ate fish, salad, noodles, *miso* soup – and bread. Sometimes we have yogurt, which I don't like, or raisin bread, which I *really* don't like. I love hamburgers, but Japanese food is the best!'

'I'm Moe Yokota. I'm 9, too. I didn't have anything for breakfast this morning – I overslept. I think this happens to a lot of people. Sometimes my mother serves creamed rice for breakfast, and I don't like that anyway. My favourite Japanese food of all is usually eaten at dinnertime, in the evening. It's *sushi* – raw fish served with rice.'

8 Changes at Work

Company loyalty

The Japanese word *samurai* means 'one who serves'. From the twelfth to the nineteenth centuries, *samurai* worked faithfully for the rich lords who paid them. They were fierce warriors and followed a strict code of conduct that emphasized the qualities of loyalty, bravery and endurance. It has been said that today's hard-working Japanese company employee is the modern-day *samurai*.

Working for a large company in Japan is more than just a job. The company is part of almost everything a worker does. Many workers awaken each morning in a house, apartment or dormitory room that is paid for by the company. The company will provide a pass for the train or bus for each employee to travel to work, or pay for the petrol if a car is driven. At the office or factory, the day will probably start with group exercises before work begins.

Companies often plan weekend trips away for groups of employees to help promote team spirit. On special occasions, workers sing company songs together.

▼ *These business people in Kamakura have visited a temple. Even people who are very busy still make time for traditional Japanese rituals.*

IN THEIR OWN WORDS

'My name is Makiko Sato. I work for a big pharmaceutical company in Tokyo. I'm a secretary. I like my work, and I'm lucky because I live only twenty minutes' walk from the office. The job I had before was terrible. I was an editor for a book publisher. I'd start at nine in the morning and often wouldn't arrive home until after midnight. I worked a lot of Saturdays and Sundays, too.

'There is a good atmosphere in the office I work in now. We often go out together after work, and sometimes the company organizes social occasions. I think I could find another job if I wanted to, but I like working here!'

Before and after work, company pins are worn to show which company a worker is part of. Workers will often socialize late into the night with people they know from their job. Often company life seems to be more important than family or personal life.

A strong sense of company loyalty will continue to be an important part of work in Japan, but in the twenty-first century, there will be more and more people whose work will not be as significant in shaping every part of their lives.

▶ *These workers in Tokyo are enjoying a game of* pachinko – *a kind of pinball game – after work. Even with all the new electronic video games, this old-fashioned mechanical game is still very popular.*

Women at work

Traditionally, the only company job available to many women was in a factory or as an office lady, or OL. For many years, the work of OLs consisted mainly of serving tea to the male workers in the office and making photocopies. Most OLs would find a husband within the company, and by age 25 would leave work to become homemakers and take care of their husbands. In recent years, however, the Japanese government has passed laws that make it easier for women to work at more responsible jobs within companies. There are now more female managers in Japan than ever before, and their numbers are steadily increasing.

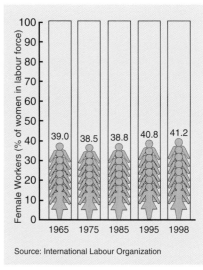

Source: International Labour Organization

▲ Although women in Japan are doing a greater variety of jobs than ever before, the percentage of women in the workforce is increasing very slowly.

◄ This busy woman is working during her coffee break.

The number of couples in Japan with both the husband and the wife working in jobs outside of the home is also increasing. When there are no children, the couples can enjoy the extra money from two paycheques. When there are children, however, the children need to be taken care of during the day. In most cases, the working wife is responsible for making arrangements for this and for taking care of the children when the family is at home.

▲ *This office lady, or OL, works for a large manufacturing company near Osaka.*

IN THEIR OWN WORDS

'My name is Naoko Ikeda. I work part-time as a presenter on the radio in the city of Nara. The best part of my job is doing research. Before I talk about something on the radio, I need to learn about it myself. Once, we did a programme about local food shops, so of course I had to visit all of them and taste everything. That was great!

'I'm really lucky – when my mother was young there weren't many opportunities for women to work, especially after they were married. Nowadays, married women like me often have jobs. I really enjoy my work!'

Changes in manufacturing

Manufacturing, especially of cars, electrical goods and steel, has been very important to Japan in the past. But as a result of changes in Japan's economy, only 21 per cent of the workforce now work in manufacturing jobs, compared with 36 per cent in 1970. Just over 5 per cent of the total now work in agriculture. The remaining 74 per cent work as everything from shop assistants to bankers, and also as artists.

Artists

Art has always been an important part of Japanese society. Actors in *kabuki*, a type of traditional Japanese theatre, are famous all over the country and are very well paid. All *kabuki* actors are male, even the ones who play female characters. They make dramatic entrances and exits on a ramp that runs right through the audience. The music is loud and the stories are exciting.

◄ *These women are called* geishas. *They are professional entertainers, highly trained in traditional music, dance and art.*

A skilled artist of any kind is addressed with the respectful title of *sensei*, which means 'skilled master'. The title *sensei* is also given to doctors, priests, teachers and politicians.

Pottery-making is another traditional art that is very important in Japanese culture. The history of pottery-making in Japan goes back thousands of years. The work of master potters is very highly valued even in today's high-tech world.

Another kind of artist in Japan is a calligrapher. Calligraphy is the art of using pens or brushes to produce beautiful writing. Written Japanese characters are so complex and beautiful, that writing them well is considered an art, like painting.

Many people believe that Japan has an almost perfect balance of old traditions and new developments.

▶ *Practising the art of calligraphy is a popular hobby amongst the Japanese.*

IN THEIR OWN WORDS

'My name is Yoko Nishina and my son's name is Shuya. I'm a calligrapher and a calligraphy teacher. I live in Kyoto. I make less money than an OL, but I'm more free. This is important to me, because I want to spend as much time as I can with my son. My hope for him is that he will find something in life that he loves to do, like I have. I love the quiet atmosphere of a calligraphy class. To do calligraphy, your mind must be quiet and calm. It's a pity that most people use a computer for all kinds of writing, now. People don't write by hand as much anymore. I love the feeling of the brush on the paper as I form the letters. That's something really special.'

Commuting

It's an amazing fact that 10 million people in Tokyo all travel to work in the city centre at about the same time every morning. Japan's public transport system is the most efficient in the world. Every day, about two million commuters pass through Tokyo's Shinjuku Station alone. There are dozens of busy train stations in central Tokyo, but Shinjuku is one of the busiest train stations in the world. Here, in the height of the morning rush hour, between 7:30 am and 9:30 am, ropes are stretched across the entrances to the train platforms to limit the number of people on the platform at any one time.

▶ *At the height of the rush hour in Tokyo, trains are so crowded that commuters have to be pushed inside by people called* oshiya *('pusher') so that the doors can close.*

IN THEIR OWN WORDS

'My name is Naoko Umemoto. My journey to work is about average, I guess – a little more than an hour on the train. People who get on near the beginning of the train line are able to find a seat, but I have to stand. It's crazy, when you think about it, everyone being packed into trains like sardines. One time, I was pushed and shoved so much that my shoe came off and fell between the platform and the train. I had to call for an attendant to come and get it out for me! It was an expensive shoe, and I was on my way to work, so what could I do? I had to have it.'

On busy lines, trains may come as often as once every 90 seconds. They quickly fill with commuters, and packed into the trains, many workers and students travel standing up for an hour or more. The average commuting time for workers in Tokyo is 90 minutes. Some people may try to read a book or a newspaper, but most trains are so crowded in the rush hour that listening to music on a personal stereo is the easiest option. Many people have learned to sleep, or at least rest, while standing!

Not everyone takes the train to work. People who work outside of the central business districts may take a bus or drive their own car. Others are able to ride bicycles or even walk. Some companies build dormitories for their workers so that they are able to live closer to the factories where they work.

▼ *This two-level bike rack outside a Yokohama train station is a good solution to the problem of space. Many people cycle to their local train station as the first part of their commute.*

9 The Way Ahead

The early twenty-first century has been a difficult time for the Japanese economy. In the mid-1990s, the strong economic growth of the 60s, 70s and 80s ended. Japan is still a leading manufacturer and exporter of products such as cars, computers and cameras, but it isn't as easy as it used to be. In the second half of the twentieth century, Japanese companies made their products in Japan, sold them abroad and made a lot of money. Since the 1980s, they have begun building more factories outside of Japan in the United States, the UK, Europe and South-east Asia, to save money. Unemployment in Japan has begun to increase.

An old Japanese proverb says, 'A rock will become warm if you sit on it for three years.' The meaning of the proverb is that success will come to you if you work at a problem for long enough. The new problems that Japan faces today will need to be solved by the strength of the Japanese people, with their long history and old traditions and with new ideas. Today's Japan is a place where the very old and the very new exist side-by-side.

▼ *These traditional Japanese folded paper cranes were sent to the Hiroshima Peace Park by a school class in Florida, USA. Paper cranes have become an international symbol of peace.*

Ms. Altstatt's
World Cultures Classes
Callahan Middle School
Callahan, Florida USA

1st Period

5th Period

IN THEIR OWN WORDS

'My name is Kosei Morimoto. I'm a Buddhist monk. I live and work in one of Japan's largest and most famous temples, called *Todaiji*, in the city of Nara. Thirty years ago, young people all wanted to gain entry to the best universities. It was very important to find a good job, to make a lot of money. People wanted to work a lot to make a good life. Young people today already live in a wealthy nation, so they don't need to work so hard for things. Working isn't so important today. My hope is that as work becomes less important, young people will find a new direction, instead of just playing all of the time. I hope they find a way to do something good – and meaningful – for themselves and for the world.'

For example, ancient celebrations associated with the changing seasons are still a part of everyday life. Some people say balancing old and new is becoming more difficult, and that young people are less and less likely to understand the old ways. The challenge will be for Japan to continue holding on to a rich past while taking full advantage of the changes of the future.

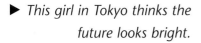

▶ *This girl in Tokyo thinks the future looks bright.*

Glossary

Agriculture Farming the land and producing food.

Ancestors Members of your family who lived in the past.

Birth rate The number of people born in a given area over a period of time.

Calligraphy The art of beautiful writing with a brush.

Consumer Someone who buys or uses goods and services.

Dormitory A large building where many people live together.

Economy All the business activity in a country.

Efficient Working well, without wasting time or energy.

Endangered species An animal or plant that may not exist in the near future.

Haori A traditional Japanese jacket.

Hydroelectric power The force of falling water used to generate electricity.

Import To buy goods from other countries.

Judo A traditional Japanese sport in which two opponents try to push each other to the ground.

Karaoke Singing to recorded music for entertainment.

Karate A traditional Japanese sport of unarmed fighting.

Kendo A traditional Japanese sport in which two opponents try to hit one another with wooden swords.

Kimono A traditional Japanese dress.

Land reclamation Taking land from one place to another in order to create a new area of land.

Life expectancy How long people in a particular area live on average.

Livestock Animals that are kept on a farm.

Mineral A naturally occurring rock, such as coal.

Monk A male member of a religious group.

Nuclear power Electricity made from the energy of splitting atoms.

Obesity The condition of being so overweight that it is bad for your health.

Polar ice-caps The ice at the North and South Poles.

Population The total number of people in a place at a given time.

Richter scale A way of measuring the strength of earthquakes.

Redundant Without a job because a company has too many employees and not enough work.

Samurai A member of a powerful military class in Japan in past times.

Scuba-diving The sport of swimming underwater, breathing air from a container worn on your back.

Shinto The ancient religion of Japan that involves the worship of nature and of ancestors.

Staple The food that is normally eaten.

Subtropical A subtropical area is an area near a tropical region that has a warm climate.

Temple A religious building.

Typhoon A strong, windy storm.

Urban An urban area is built-up, such as a town or a city.

Further Information

Books

The Adventure of Momotaro, the Peach Boy by Ralph F. McCarthy (Kodansha Europe, 2000)

Naomi: The Strawberry Blonde of Pippu Town by Karmel Schreyer (Great Plains Fiction, 1999)

Sadako and the Thousand Paper Cranes by Eleanor Coerr (Putnam, 1999)

Discover Japan by the Japan Culture Institute (Kodansha Europe, 1999)

Today's Japan Illustrated (Japan Travel Bureau, 1999)

Videos

Nippon, The Land and Its People Number 1: The tradition of performing arts in Japan

Nippon, The Land and Its People Number 2: The Japanese businessman

Nippon, The Land and Its People Number 3: The Japanese family

Nippon, The Land and Its People Number 4: The tastes of Japan

Nippon, The Land and Its People Number 5: Japanese technology

Nippon, The Land and Its People Number 6: Japanese society

Nippon, The Land and Its People Number 7: Customs and manners

Nippon, The Land and Its People Number 8: The Japanese and nature

Nippon, The Land and Its People Number 9: Japan's corporate system

Nippon, The Land and Its People Number 10: Education in Japan

Nippon, The Land and Its People Number 11: Working women

Nippon, The Land and Its People Number 12: Annual festivities and ceremonies (Nippon Steel Human Resources)

Websites

Hiroshima Peace Site:
http://www.pcf.city.hiroshima.jp/peacesite

Kidsweb Japan:
http://www.jinjapan.org/kidsweb

Japan for Visitors, Japan Travel Guide:
http://www.gojapan.about.com

Japan Etcetera:
http://www.welcome.to/japan-etcetera

Sadako and the Thousand Paper Cranes:
http://www.sadako.com

Useful Addresses

Japan National Tourist Organization,
Heathcoat House,
20 Savile Row,
London W1S 3PR
Tel: 020 7734 9638
Website: http://www.tourist-offices.org.uk/Japan

Japanese Embassy in the United Kingdom,
101-104 Piccadilly,
London W1J 7NJ
Tel: 020 7465 6500
Website: http://www.embjapan.org.uk

Japanese Embassy in Australia,
112 Empire Circuit,
Yarralumla,
ACT 2600
Tel: (02) 6273 3244
Website: http://www.japan.org.au

Index